ZEPPELIN

zeppelin

blaise moritz

NIGHTWOOD EDITIONS

2013

Nightwood Editions
P.O. Box 1779
Gibsons, BC V0N 1V0
Canada
www.nightwoodeditions.com

TYPOGRAPHY & COVER DESIGN: Carleton Wilson

Nightwood Editions acknowledges financial support from the Government of Canada
through the Canada Book Fund and the Canada Council for the Arts, and from the
Province of British Columbia through the British Columbia Arts Council and the Book
Publisher's Tax Credit.

This book has been produced on 100% post-consumer recycled, ancient-forest-free
paper, processed chlorine-free and printed with vegetable-based dyes.

Printed and bound in Canada.

LIBRARY AND ARCHIVES CANADA CATALOGUING IN PUBLICATION

Moritz, Blaise
Zeppelin / Blaise Moritz.

Poems.
ISBN 978-0-88971-279-9

I. Title.

PS8576.O725Z44 2013   C811'.6   C2012-908423-9

To the crew

CONTENTS

An old photo of the Zeppelin that Goodyear flew out of Akron,

airship nose poking from massive hangar archway:

immediately, I'm charmed by the image,

its antique tones, its steampunk and surrealism.

Then I picture myself among the airmen and mechanics,

tiny foreground figures subsumed beneath the metal balloon,

the Zeppelin's leviathan scale and factory roar akin

to all I hate or ignore in our present moment.

Vain Zeppelin, I want to understand your transmutation:

monumental and advanced, you vanished,

only to reappear as a thing available to utopian visions.

When I was a toddler, I'm told, we were picnicking on a bluff

and found ourselves magically level with another airship,

moored at the lakeshore below. In false memory now

I'm eye to eye with you, astonishing fellow creature.

I T

With no necessary death point
it struggled to ongo, rather than lapse
into a final, inescapable torpor.

Yes, the atmosphere might turn
to boiling soup; cold extreme
enough to thwart its capacity
to clothe itself might blow in;
more likely: nothing would ever kill it.

And so its every instant was not simply
respiration, locomotion, excretion
but an act of will.

SHAWARMA

In the porn blue, a construction, fibrous and motivational
revolves in the window above rain puddles that form

in vales of knobbly asphalt between small peaks
scoured by rolling tires — rubber glaciers that draggle

unread and uneaten particles of yesterday's version
of your city. A vulgarly mouth-watering hock,

it towers before you, naked and damned, warmed on a spit
taller than the world's tallest free-standing structure,

the folds of its growing body glistening with healthless
grease. A slice will be taken for a mere five dollars,

six with a drink, to sustain your day's work, after which,
this animal, for it seems alive on its rotisserie,

this carcass, for it is not alive, this building,
for it has been assembled by hand, a thing neither reared

and slaughtered, nor cultivated and harvested,
will exude enough new matter for all tomorrow's lunches.

THE DISHWASH SUN

The dishwash sun greyed upon its rise,
rid of yellow burn, a sun not of fire
but of fur. We shivered amidst our stolen

chickens—reduced to begging, what else
were we to eat? We almost despaired
of him, but at last he emerged—

it had taken him days to reach us,
groping along narrow paths left between
countless bundles of old newspapers

in the place he was building for himself:
"Its walls will be for reading," he declared,
joining the group. Scummy, scudless,

the cloudy leftovers overhead were typically
decrepit yet opaque enough to obscure
the work of the minute-taker. Our meat

cooked unevenly, the rotisserie wobbling
along the crumpled terrain. We became
nostalgic for a house that bowed,

where everything rolled into the middles
of rooms. Nearby, a gully once had careened
down to a trickling crick, gentle but dogged

current, fully expressed in the centre
of that house: debris, furniture, people
all flowing out the front door. "Now

that house is all dried up," lamented cook,
squeezing a black leg to test for foam
and to see if the flesh was soft enough.

CITY UNDER AN EPIDEMIC

Like the stalks of certain flowers,
the glass column swells into a globe
partway up its height; it identifies

the storefront to the passers-by
as do pawnshop spheres and striped poles:
a pharmacy. The vessel in this one's window

is filled with liquid coloured to tell
the health of the city. It speaks in code
like the stack of ring-shaped neon tubes

high atop the tallest building, that shows
by hues and patterned alternations
temperature, humidity, types of precipitation.

The city is characterized by information
and by the delightful contrivances that create it.

The pharmacist's globe is red this morning—
signal that the town is sick, in the midst
of an epidemic. Arriving early before posted

opening hours, having overheard in the streets
that hospital beds and morgue slabs
continue to be full, the pharmacist mixes

ferrous oxide and a little grenadine with water
and fills the globe, no eagerness for the traffic
this advertisement will attract. Other colours—

for hangover, malaise, even for health—
call not for cures, but restoratives, tonics
and delicacies, all of which are mixed here.

The shop is a city of finely built glass towers
each housing its particular ingredient.

Minerals, in powder and crystal, plant matter,
dried and fresh, animal products, trapped
gasses, some elements as yet unused:

the pharmacist's first art is to identify
substances which may be ingested, always
expanding the possibilities of confection.

Later, plague victim and apothecary consult
the palate that's been assembled, font
of medicines but also of soft drinks,

assemblage of means to health and sweetness,
and cabinet of curiosities of a material world
before the descent into the molecular or atomic.

Trade in potions and serums is brisk, with red
in the window day after day, and the city emptying.

I SAW A MAN OF BLOOD

I saw a man of blood who hadn't been overtaken
walking erect and red amidst the iron trees
of a construction site, pausing to mark all struts
and lintels soon to be bathed in rich concrete.

Those who'd inherited hauling stones didn't see
how grease and dry bits of skin had shifted
from their hands to the exposed innards
of the body they were hammering together.

Over what they were building, he spat his curses,
bent on persisting within its finishes and tenants.

BEAUTIFUL PEOPLE

Beautiful people's interchangeable body parts
are bagged up in the backs of many closets,
unwanted toys. Many pieces have gone missing,
small pieces—fingernails, tips of noses—
those are always the first to go.

If you have one of these persons in its entirety,
you've really got something and should bring it down
to the auction, if you're keeping it only out of sentiment,
and have no intention of playing with it again.

OLD POLONIUS

You wanted my cheek, I gave you my coat.
Walk one more mile, walk one more mile.
A tooth for an eye and I still see
and still have thirty-one teeth, I won't
resist you, but as for change, I gave
it all to the guy right outside the station.
You can't condemn me for refusing you,
my right hand didn't know what my left
was doing and that was all I had...
                                        Old
Polonius, dear Polonius, what advice
will get us out of this hole?
They're heaping stones upon us;
would that we could be as he is,
the one who takes such stones and eats
them as bread. "A book is like a wilderness,"
you told me, "a desert, with its mirage."
I have seen the apparent reflection in a wet
stretch of superhighway when the sun
is scorching. "I've been stung," I exclaimed
once but it wasn't a scorpion after all—
I'd been dreaming.
                        Alone in endless sands,
I stopped suddenly, yielding
to indistinct creatures scuttling across my path,
creatures who, in the logic of that place,
I then identified as phrases:

every bit of wisdom I'd treasured. I woke
wondering how I hadn't recognized them
at once.

       "Yes, yes," you smiled
like a teacher excited that a student breaks
through at last, "that's the sting!"

A WILDERNESS IN THE DIVINE LOVE

There is a wilderness in the divine love,
where the concrete of the universe shows
signs of wear and biting, where once
we found a dental mould of a creature

with two mouths—one for liquid food
and one for solid. Not the most
unusual species of angel we came upon
in that clime: others with bodies as flat

as paper were continually sliding against
one another, their sex, insertion of tab A
into slot B. In the local tongue, words
were spoken in the form of dew, the verbose

prized for their contributions to irrigation.
Watery chats flowed up flights of stairs,
threatening the upper stories of the hotel
where we had our rooms. The sun there

seems a ball of yarn, uncoiling
a burning strand onto the earth, which,
with mouth puckered as if about a straw,
inhales the warmth to fill its core,

the heat rising up beneath visiting toes,
steaming conversations. There's a word
on the lips of this desert, a word that fails
in its purpose, that remains a white film

almost dried up on the lips and on the teeth,
passive and sick smelling. Eyes wrinkled
like raisins, unblinking, spied in at us
from a face the consistency of plaster.

TWO WOMEN

What's the difference between the dead and those who never lived?
Memory preserves fictions and real events equally.

My bones are in the ground, says the dead woman,
surely that counts for something. I'm hidden, but not lost.
Dig up the spine curved by long years stooped,
dragging or pushing my wire cart between house and market.
Like a bus, I had my route, back and forth on schedule.
Check around where I lived. If they haven't torn up the sidewalk
to work underground and left it all patched with blacktop,
there's bound to be some sign of wear. Like a river, I coursed
along the same line, deepening it, bending it slightly over time.
I was a natural force.

From her book, a woman who has never lived continues
to speak. Does she speak when the book is closed?
Open it a fraction of an inch to see if the lights are on:
does the automaton go perpetually or is there some switch
triggered by the movement of the covers? I remember
meeting her as a child, the sun white, the aperture could never
be small enough to avoid overexposure. She was the same age then,
beautiful, poised on the verge of hateful decay, innocence
cracking, betraying a few indications of how her character was
to sour. And she is still there, at that crux.

THE FLAMBOYANT DICTIONARY

The flamboyant dictionary sacrificed meaning
for the glamour of real teeth,
tiger's teeth,
glued into mouths of illustrations
of the largest cat species.

On opening the current single volume edition,
massive in its external dimensions,
one finds all inner pages hollowed out,
and no content
other than a magnificent life-sized sculpture,
head of a Siberian tiger,
still with the now-trademarked *Real Teeth*.

DURING THE FLOOD

Then the stalls were filled with the clean beasts by sevens, the male
    and his female,

and with beasts that are not clean by two, fleshed forms made in
    secret,

intricately woven in the depths of the earth, wonderful works that
    no one

had ever had such opportunity to inspect. Noah and his sons and his
    wife and his sons' wives,

as the waters prevailed, sat and watched the living creatures, asleep
    and bestirred,

and drew them. They drew the lions, at first only as others had, not
    lions

but hieroglyphs, flat outlines filled with gold, stylized manes and
    forelimbs

raised rampant. But in that long scrutiny, in its occasional
    wordlessness,

the symbol disappeared, its place emptied except for light, volume,
    texture and anatomy.

MAKHMALBAF ON THE IRANIAN CINEMA

Prelude

A jagged horizon: the arid mountains
of eastern Iran painted flat. Beneath
orientalized trunks and leaves, a royal
Persian tiger in an ochre field. But now
    we're after the revolution…

1

On screen,
    the executioner begins to doubt his blind faith,
and you're crying,
    alone in a little lab in Italy,
ashamed of the mediocre retelling of his story.

He didn't watch the movie
    but seized the negative, made you leave;
long hours of shooting without artificial light
    were lost, what little you saved
on computer you've brought here
    to make a second version.

Next project:
    the story of a painter condemned
for using peasants as models for his saints.
    "It's about an artist fleeing the Inquisition,"
you tell the interviewer matter-of-factly,
    just a newspaper reporter

so the analogy doesn't strike him as heavy-handed—
    it'll be better on film.

2

Either too mysterious or too simple—
    it's always one or the other—
when they try to explain us. We're not as strange
    or subtle as some suppose.
With them, I always wonder:

can the stories they're used to really be so plain?

A story within a story—
    such as delighted the Satraps left behind by Alexander—
is, for them, a sign of the too-modern world,
    a derangement of the senses.
But we can get along with them, at least:
    the innocents, unsure, but they laugh,
they "relate to" wanting to be played by someone good-looking.

It's the others who vex us:
    "…virtue from necessity. Their style,
artful and oblique, beloved of cineastes everywhere…
    unexpected byproduct of censorship."
A moment of experience,
    the premiere of my own story:

"Bravo to the director! But bravo also to dictators
    who give the artist painful memories to transform!
See, they won't even let him forget,
    won't permit him to make his film, *Amnesia!*"

There was no library in the prison
    where I lived five years, without poetry
except what I could remember.
    Payami, Fahmanara, Bahari, Kiarostami,
all that we say, and how we say it, is there
    in centuries of verse, in the *qasida*,

occasional song of praise or invective,
    an elegy or meditation,
a supple form, almost anything really,
    as long as it runs over fifteen lines,

and the main subject is something other than love.

AT THE VENETIAN

Canals glisten beneath faux Adriatic
skies. Here it's always dusk, the time when people
spend the most according to the consultants
retained by Las Vegas Sands Inc., developers
of The Venetian. Well over a billion
dollars to implode the old Rat Pack hangout
and replicate Piazza
San Marco on the strip, the Campanile
complete with fifteen-foot crowning statue
of Gabriel, and for the disappointed
gamblers a new Bridge of Sighs.
The would-be Doges, walled in with marble
quarried from the Old World pit,
win paltry hundreds at the tables, later
retire to cramped luxury suites, merchant
princes, not tourists, talking on the bathroom
phone or bossing gondoliers
under contract to remain in character. I'm
staying in Paris this trip
but there's no romance to this place either.
The Eiffel Tower done at half-size, the Arc de Triomphe
at two-thirds—and besides, I've been a flâneur
in the real thing, for four days
when I was seven, four days I remember
beautifully: the heat as we walked, mother
and son, the entire length of the city.
The concierge served warm milk,
a man greeted a lady with two kisses,
I ordered us Cokes in French.

*

I can't see myself as a Doge. A worker
out of work—once I built an imitation
palace but now it's done...only authentic
in terms of my labour. In a low-lying
industrial shed on one of those unsuspected
streets beyond the airport, I might've punched in
for my shift and carved ornamental designs
into Styrofoam, following patterns printed
on raw blocks from scanned photos—
the Corinthian foliage of a capital,
a pedimental lion's
stylized mane—step one in a process, patent
pending, used to fake all kinds
of old hand-cut masonry. Or maybe
I'd have answered a come-on in the Vegas
daily to earn extra rent and paint money,
played Michangelo
on scaffolding above the galleria,
traced frescoes—Veronese,
Bambini, Tiepolo—around the sprinklers,
smoke eaters and muzak speakers required in
that ceiling. Or I might have made the countless
research trips to Italy,
one of those artists hired to sketch sites chosen
for replication over in Nevada—
I would've seen Venice, not The Venetian,
that way. My afternoon off
from frigid meeting rooms, I've come
to watch the gondolas of the desert.

TO MARTIAL

What interests me are the fifteen years

between the execution of Lucan and Seneca,
your fellow Spaniards and benefactors
upon your arrival in the capital,
for their complicity in an imperial assassination plot,

and the publication of your *Liber Spectaculorum*,
lines written on the occasion
of the Coliseum's grand opening,

fifteen years during which you lived
in a mean third-storey apartment in Rome;

the epigrams leave me cold.

I SCAN NOT SEE THE CITY STREET

I scan not see the city street,
understand at once what might be done
inside the passing boxes, identify
where I can fulfill my needs.

I inhabit a field of symbols,
a place on earth where the mind's drift
toward simplicity—lines and lists—
has made itself madly physical.

A hill built over, a lake spoiled
and silvered, might save me: to see
some landscape, something outside
that enters me. I was an ancient once,
my sight a power I projected, in spite
of all modern accounts of optics. Now,
too late, I know my eyes are starved.

MY LITTLE CIVILIZATION

My little civilization will be in trouble one day,
bits crumbling, me, the linchpin, dying.
From some bed, I'll be forgetting all my confusion
of objects, the assemblage of which was both
spontaneity and drudgery.

                    The clutter
of my kitchen is my poem: this fork
has made it here all the way from a drawer
in rented rooms, stolen from a college apartment,
from the accumulation bequeathed
to all future generations from all those who had left.

The marks on the wall that I have made,
the blemishes to things once white,
the creases and bends in things once flat,
record my secretions, movement and growth,
passage of electricity along my nerves.
I'm beating and buzzing, marking everything
around me, giving it that prized patina
or maybe just ruining and, after dark, loading up
broken bits, bound for a dumpster I know,
where I'm able to trash stuff unobserved.

On move-out day, will there be time
to leave rooms empty and clean, to refuse any trace
of ourselves to those to come?

We erased ourselves from many places, left,
uncelebrated, but always at the price of driving late
into the night, into the void of unlit highways,
reflective sticks at the roadside clicking off
distance and time that might never end,
we might always be driving, all that we had chosen
to keep loaded onto us, the U-Haul our snail shell, the cab
our body, the two of us, piloting, the antennae.

This was life in eternity:
moving forward lugging our stuff, things no longer webbed
together by echoing rationalizations:
shelves for books...rooms for shelves...
houses for rooms...cities for houses...
the earth for cities...
the earth, which some claim predates us by billions of years.

THE DEATH OF ROBERT LOWELL

Dramatis Personae

Robert Lowell
A cab driver

SCENE: *In a cab, en route from Kennedy Airport to West 67th*

Actors sit facing the audience, the cab driver addressing Lowell behind him, though staring out at us, as through the windshield of the car. Lowell's speeches are pre-recorded and played through speakers, the audience hearing his backseat musings, as he remains, to the cab driver, silent. The cabbie never ceases chattering, and the speeches should fade in and out of each other, with the lights on the driver dimming when we hear Lowell's voice.

  Cabbie.   If there's to be no now and forever
it'd be better for you to live without vows.
I'm not trying to censor your changing heart
but enough already of these protestations
that your heart unchanging
this time for sure has found its eternity
in some new love or new god or new mode
of expression. It's false drama
if it's just a man's unquiet desperation —
as if quiet were despair. What you want
is election, and that's where you get your ethic:
to make a show of virility, of protean
power. You're too large to be anything
but restless with systems —
marriage, religion, poetry, et cetera, et cetera.
(*After a pause, with a check of the mirror*)

How're you doing back there?
Taking this all in? It's good stuff.
Seriously, aren't you ever embarrassed
to look back, to think of the names
you've burned through, the people
you've named stars for, then later
turned on and tried to blot from heaven
as if their accumulations of words could be either
saintly or diabolical?

Lowell.   I never look back.
I must go forward, always. Who knows
how far it is to the surface and sunlight,
who knows if she still follows behind.
Perhaps I've been mocked and even now
am alone, singing to no one as I grope along.

Cabbie.   Memory is the coming thing
but there's all kinds of memory.
Cultural memory—"the books are filled
with the names of kings,"
but what about the workers, right? What
about me? And what do you do with that
kind of memory anyway? It mesmerizes you
like the Aleph in which you see the whole world
but all you can do is look and look. Bad
for poetry too, the meditative murmur
that comes out of the sense of grasping
all. Seems an otherworldly, dreamlike
beauty for a while, but it gets monotonous.
Then there's personal memory: "Forgive
me, Father, for I have sinned."
And you imagine all the world saying,

"Do tell." But a litany of sins,
however titillating at first, soon raises the question
of relevance, and a confession is something else
entirely. You take "Father" and "forgiveness"
out and I guess you're left clinging to biography,
that most instructive art.

    Lowell.   It was a great adventure
and my power was song. There were others
to fight, but only me to sing.
I could inspire them, I could soothe them,
I could protect them from other songs, the fatal
songs that made shipwreck beauty — but
did we survive or was it just a song
I made up of another brave escape
from the impossible trap? It seems to me
now I see the beach littered with the timbers
of the hull and the bones of the crew,
all bleached and weathered, and my bones
there among them.

    Cabbie.   But what can I learn
from you? I'd say the century
of revolutions is ending, and disillusionment
too. See over there on the left —
on the other side of those hoardings
is where they're putting up those new towers.
Going to be the tallest in the world.
They had to knock down ten blocks
to prepare the site. I read they demolished
something called the Hudson Terminal Buildings.
Never noticed it myself, not a lot of fares
in this vicinity, but I guess that's about to change.

Anyway, these buildings were finished back in 1908,
identical twenty-two-storey "skyscrapers," the tallest
in Manhattan, for all of fourteen months.
You could write an ode to the new towers,
their visionary engineers, the miraculous materials,
the spectacle of human might and courage,
the men who work straddling a beam
a hundred storeys above the earth,
make its upward thrust a symbol,
or you could write an elegy on the constant
erasure of the former city, see collaboration
with death in all this upheaval.
Either way, there's a narrative.
A story, I'd say, depends on the tragic flaws
of its narrator for its action.
But when you've seen the story play out
again and again, the tragic momentum
comes off as rigged with plot devices.
What patience can today's audience
have for yet another intellectual's or artist's
mid-life conversion or happy beginning
to a second marriage? We can see
how it's going to end and instead
of being moved—and sometimes a Christ
or an Oedipus can still have some impact—
we're sitting there right at the conversion
or the wedding saying, "Don't do it!"

Lowell.   But I've no comfort except for song,
and my songs have charmed. Alone now,
having lost all, having spent my experience
of epic and of the world of the dead,
I go on singing to pass the time.

My first life having already produced its outcome,
I live my second, sing to the inanimate
world, the apartment floor, the old
subway rattling far below, but I'm not there...
still in Rome...no, in the wild solitudes
of my own country...they come to tear
me apart, drop, drop in silence, then
a louder drop, echoed...My head
is floating down this river of cars...
that's funny, Lizzie...

Cabbie. (*Standing on the brakes and turning to look in the backseat.*)
                          Jesus,
are you okay? Come on, Mr. Lowell,
you can't die in my damned cab!

Curtain.

ACROSS THE GRID

Across the grid, ravines curl,
curl enough to seem improbably large
and disorient a straight-line traveller.

I've felt terror down
by a trickle through dead leaves, down
in the shade of the high canopy
of hundreds of thin-trunked weeds shooting for sun.
And following that curl, surprised
that the steps back up to the street
still aren't in sight, I've despaired,
and imagined myself fantastically lost.

Terror: what have I known
but the city's protection? The love
I have for nature is within
front and back yards, zoological gardens.
A little subdued scrub,
topographically inconvenient to pave,
is where I felt the menace
that first set us clearing and building.

ECLOGUE

Why sing of buildings, of blocks razed
for condos? That's what I have: species
of rectangle and construction machinery,

observations on proportions and materials,
the way a layperson learns tower-raising
techniques over the course of a city life.

I have no woods, no wild birds, unless
I go elsewhere to seek them out,
so that I too may sing of wild birds and woods.

I'm with you, says the house sparrow,
from her perch on a leafless grey stalk,
a city tree jutting from a hole in the pavement.

The world's different than it was, and I'd like
to be sung to in new idioms, no more laments
for the colourful natives I supplant,

no more odes to me as representative
of indomitable nature. Where else can I go?
If you retreat to pastoral tradition

or perceived wilderness, I can't follow.
I have no poet, no song, unless
you stay to seek your fate with me.

WHILE THE CONTINENT OF USERS
IS DREAMING

While the continent of users is dreaming,
the programmers, unknown, are writing code,
sweating at the workstations of a mausoleum
in the antipodes, beyond the equatorial fire,
bewildering verses in an ugly dialect, thick
with punctuation marks and nonsense words,
subroutines supremely functional yet full of bugs,
line after line of dot matrix characters
printed on long sheets banded white and green
or white and orange, folded accordion-style
to stack, a skyscraper-high epic, its theme
stated and restated: calculations show
there's neither will nor means to build anymore
except on screens, except with language.

ULYSSES

Tonight again I cross the stream of Ocean
without Eurylochus, without Perimedes.
Remember, they were lost. All lost. Alone
I had my homecoming. Well in order
at the oarlocks new mariners pull me
toward...what? None of you will become
a name as I have. Even now you lose
your names, mere devices of my return
to wandering. I found purpose early,
hungered, travelled, piled life on life. Maybe
I shouldn't have. I've known the strength that makes
age worse, incapacity worse. How I must
intimidate you. The lines on my face,
my gaze, my tone, my movements, the richness
of all I am. I don't envy you your youth,
full of intimations, of strength never
to be exercised. Later the unanswerable,
why wasn't I Ulysses?

THE PORT OF LONDON

Ocean-going, diesel-powered,
containerized and automated,
ships land at deep-watered,
downriver Tilbury.

The Port of London now
far removed from the City,
invisible to those whose goods it processes,
forever rolling on, rolling off,
deafening noise turned to silence—

protective headphones cancel everything
for the scant staff atomized about the yard:
ten storeys up, a toy operator
in the crane's control booth;
far below, the progress of an ant
whose shift has ended toward the car park.

No need for the morning call,
for crowds at the gates.
Heyday of the man-sized parcel
when all was muscle,
no one word for what was handled:
cask, crate, bail, bundle
spool, jug, barrel, sack.
And the uncontainable:
double-decker buses bound for Ceylon,
an elephant imported for the zoo.

IF THE CHILD COULD BE A CHILD ALWAYS

If the child could be a child always,
it would save many things once loved innocently,
and only later rejected.
It might save not only the monkey bars
moulded into the form of a fire engine
but also the birdless playground,
perhaps even the institutions in which it lived,
always lined up, to go in or come out,
where there were procedures for everything —
eating time and sleeping time —
where play was a matter of things
catalogued in boxes,
taken down for a spell then tidied up and put away.

If the child could be a child always
it would not wish to be fed forever
on the universe of myths
in which it first sought fellowship:
in a nightmare,
the hero meets his skull-masked nemesis
in a landscape of hellfire, and relives
the tragic end of his sidekick, then, waking,
he takes the place of a mysterious prisoner
to foil an equally mysterious assassin.
It might keep the comic, touchstone
of early desire, taped together,
but still pick through that universe,
wishing only the best of it to endure.

If the child could be a child always
it would not allow a junk heap
to pass for material culture.
It would remember a Lego city,
boldly coloured, blocky, bright,
undiluted by toy soldiers or Matchbox cars,
but eventually clashing with the carpet
and the chrome tubing of a sofa leg.
It would be inclined toward the austere
visions of great builders.

If the child could be a child always,
it would speak to the janitor every morning
in the hallways, speak to him
in his own language for the smile
he smiles, without fear of punishment.
It would delight in speaking wisely
to the barber and keep in its pocket
three quarters, a dime, two nickels and five pennies.
The child would be able to make exact change
for any sum as the barber had taught it.
The child would wish for a small stretch
of old red-brick road laid by dim ancestors
in a faraway town, never to be repaved.

If the child could be a child always,
it would travel downtown
to the conservatory for piano lessons,
and the building would be as it was:
at the end of the hallway
where the child waits by a studio door,
a window onto a small dark shaft.
And after each afternoon session, the child

would be released at just the right moment
to see an owl—strangely out by day—
perch briefly on the shaded ledge,
never missing the enchanting bird, no matter
how long or late the lesson.

If the child could be a child always,
it would never put aside longing
for that peaceable kingdom
where knowledge is as abundant as water,
where there's fulfillment
of the charmed promises of picture books,
and cave paintings, of Audubon and Rousseau,
of zoological gardens and the child's own
ark of assorted stuffed beasts.
It would never accept
the world controlled and degraded,
the limited life of the mind ascendant,
the disappearance of species.

If the child could be a child always,
it would delight in a single word,
as sound, as question, as command,
best of all, as reference
to something loved, something desired,
something remembered.
It would live close to nonsense,
without habits or prejudices to interrupt
the enjoyment of a rhyme to no purpose.
It would not rush to judgment
against an idle tune.

THE TIC-TAC-TOE-PLAYING CHICKEN

Had the tic-tac-toe-playing chicken sold out?
I remember her at the winter's fair, plying an honest trade,
a dollar in appreciation for her talent or training
to try a fingered "O" against her pecked "X"
and, having studied the sport, marvelled at her mastery
of position, the power of the corners as opposed
to the illusory value of controlling the centre—
hers was no cat's game! Could this be her, come to the strip
where the LED display in suspenseful bursts barks:
Win $100,000
Playing Tic-Tac-Toe
With a Live Chicken!
A live chicken. Today we must suspect audio-animatronics
or computer-generated imaging in all advertisements of the marvellous.

High above the seafood buffet, I surveyed the strip
from the Rio's fifty-first floor Voodoo Lounge,
Vegas a network of lights from mountain to mountain
except for the bright range along the boulevard
where like buttes the hotel towers erupt from the plane
of service alleys and low sheds, a typology immediately evident:
the original single slabs, the second-generation long-armed crosses, the
     contemporary triads,
the older hotels smooth as if over time their former stylings
have been worn away such that only the youngest facades
maintain some crowning detail, classical or byzantine or enlightenment
ornaments which must gradually erode
until the city is visible without flourish.

Everywhere repetition: thousands of near identical chambers
for the once and future honeymooners, the transient high-rollers,
for the new family gaggles in search of another sterile playworld—
could Vegas succeed in being all things to all people? Romantic,
    slutty, wholesome,
the unlikely resolutions of the pin-up girl or cheerleader in city form.
Dozens of indistinguishable halls for the slots and gaming tables,
everywhere mirror images, in the layout of hotels, of streets,
    everywhere repetition,
in structure, but also in content, except for that one cage,
which held the singular tic-tac-toe-playing chicken.

Down on Freemont, now belittled, the old Vegas,
at the home of the world's most liberal twenty-one
watching the pushing and the splitting and the doubling down,
at one dollar per longneck drinking away the interval
until everyone will rush out to the pedestrian mall that's been made
of the former mean street for the next show:
video projected up on the canopy spanning the old clubs—
anything to draw back the crowds that have forsaken the world-class
    topless girls,
the reality of their breasts for the ersatz world uptown:
New York, Paris, Venice, even Seattle,
the unsexy monumentality of it all!

Dancing up there on that faux sky like new and malformed
    constellations,
bulbous and featureless figures, wearing vests and cowboy hats,
digital cartoon production numbers to hits as ephemeral in substance
as they are indestructible in abstract; the mouthless dancers sang:
"I've got friends in low places."
My face is there in the crowd, somewhere in a digital photograph
taken by one of the party lying flat on his back

to capture the freak show above our ringèd heads.
The flash and then back to the tables, settled
in all likelihood for the dawn, all tentative
movements toward the chicken languidly deflected by a skeptical
    challenge:
what if the chicken is put to bed at some point?
They can't have the chicken out 24/7!
And what if like the lions at the MGM Grand
there is a bedtime and, instead of arriving
as I did once at the lion habitat
just before ten, when the cats disappear into their inner chambers,
to find them restively playful, clawing at their plastic tree,
eager to be off-duty and thus never more dutifully showman-like,
we were to arrive a little late, having interrupted sure and present
    diversions,
at some unpeopled nook within the casino at the Tropicana,
finding only a large board, darkened, and an empty cage, draped,
where earlier there must have been "X"s and "O"s electrically
    illuminated
and that especial chicken of mysterious genius, plotting its next move.

MOVIE MONSTER

Looking at the monster projected on the screen,
a papier mâché model in harmony with the cardboard
kingdom over which it exercises a playful reign of terror,
I think how the black and white makes cohesive
this fantasy which must in the studio have looked patchwork
and ill-coloured, how the limitations of the medium
contribute to the enduring power of these images.
To me, they're not yesterday's crap, pre-stop motion, pre-CGI,
but a vision, integral and necessarily equal to any
subsequent vision, regardless of technical advances,
realized, with that acceptance of materials that defines
the artist, by a sci-fi auteur, recognized in these latter days,
but only as a "pioneer." All cry for something beyond the modern,
something novel and alien, and have framed this criterion for their hope:
that the unreal should be indistinguishable from the real.
And what would the auteur think were he equipped
with the tools of our contemporary filmmakers, then asked
to sit through his dated masterpiece; mightn't he agree
with the genre fans that this movie is put to shame
by later effects, which reframe his bold strokes as failed graspings.
And would he too remake them, endlessly regenerating
his monsters and explosions in state-of-the-art manner,
leaving me alone to face dismissal as sentimental, contrarian
for my insistent love of his original images, in their imperfections
more perfect than the wonders of tomorrow? I've read
that in the climactic scenes, the monster's joyous rampage,
the creature's beautiful fluidity was achieved
using stand-ins, the usual matchbox towers replicated
at dollhouse scale, the place of the menacing dwarf model taken
by a man in a rubber costume. Great fun it must have been,

amok amidst that town to be destroyed. What motivation was the actor given? *You are lost in a strange and hostile place. You must erase this world if you are to build your own.*

Got it. Roll 'em, and I'll start smashing.

IN A TOY STORE WINDOW

Impossibility on display:
regiments of scaled-down soldiers from all wars,
a fleet of model cars of all makes. Thrilling rows
of playthings that can never be played with,
no one but a collector could afford them. Worse:
what imagination could be so powerful as to break
the display not just to possess these objects
but to use them, to envision the joy of a game
which would see them mismatched compared
to the perfection they share on their crystal shelf?

THE SATURDAY PENNY

A city child, I wanted what it seems a city child should want,
and loved to spend my Saturday penny lunching out alone,
a pickle "X" inscribed within my hamburger bun's circumference.

Born heir to penny histories, dreadfuls, and magic lantern shows,
to Edison's recorded sound and comics with Ben Day dots askew,
I quested to complete *The Man Called Nova*'s cosmic saga

and to hear another cut from Elmore James.
                                        A penny was my key
to the city, first to Mount Pleasant, which with its streetcar line,
two cinemas, two bookshops, Chinese takeout and fast pitch diamond

read as well as my favourite boy detective's storybook town;
later, Queen Street crowds and towers delimited my sublime.
The penny transmuted into amusements, I'd return home

to my desk in the dormer of my third-floor room, spin LPs
and draw heroes.
                        Daughter and son, I'm bound to give you in turn
money, skyscrapers, four-colour panels, electric noise.

I go on in love, but also in doubt: one day I drew instead
my panorama of rooftops and antennae, accumulation,
it seemed, of error, fulfilling no desire. How are we to make

our own world? Today, I'll keep you here with me, lay out
Calabrese salami for lunch, and have you listen
to the best old tracks and read the most thrilling tales.

ON TRANSLATING SPIDER-MAN
INTO JAPANESE

http://marvel.com/videos/563.japanese_spiderman,_episode_01

The legend of the Spider-Man:
its essence is duty tinged with guilt.
If only Peter Parker had helped the cop,
had stopped the fugitive who would turn out
to be Uncle Ben's killer…But that night
at the studio, high from his first TV spectacular,
Peter wasn't about to do anyone else's job.
Tragic paradox: the salvation he brings the world
flows from personal failure,
failure he could've avoided only if
at the critical moment he'd already attained
the nobility of purpose he begins as penance.

That our Spider-Man is named Takuya and is a young dirt bike racer
That his tousan, Dr. Yamashiro, is earth's pre-eminent astro-archaeologist
That Takuya skips a dig at a UFO crash site for a big race
That his sisters are wide-eyed and horrified but the good doctor
    understanding
That the doctor dies at the excavation at the hands of Professor Monster's
    Iron Cross Army
That the doctor had been monitoring their secret invasion of earth and
    had meant to stop it himself
That Takuya comes at last, but too late
That Yamashiro dies in Takuya's arms, his dying wish that his son should
    carry on the fight
That the Iron Cross Army includes alien ninjas

That Takuya, armed only with rage, fails in his first encounter with the
    killers
That he flees blindly into a cave his father wished to explore
That he meets there a cosmic samurai, arch foe of Professor Monster and
    exemplar of the way of the arachnid
That the samurai has waited four hundred years in hiding to find a
    worthy champion to take up his mantle
That this new master heals Takuya's wounds with the venom of a friend:
    a giant, telepathic spider
That Takuya arises with fantastic powers
That he battles another of the Iron Cross Army's principals, a dragon lady
That she attacks him with a mecho-dinosaur
That it is toy-sized at first but swells to the stature of Godzilla
That the Spider-Man defeats it with the aid of Marveller, a spaceship that
    transforms into a giant robot—

—all this is transposing of idioms.

A vigorous and good-natured hero
who also incorporates the spider's eerie attributes—
even its uncanny sense
of when you've finally gathered the courage to crush it—
here's a bold image that travels well.

Consider by contrast, the radioactive bite,
source of super-abilities in the original text:
its meaning is in the fears of those who made atom bombs
and isn't essential to the legend;
it must be restated in bringing the Spider-Man
to those on whom the bombs were dropped.

CHAPTER III: THE BROWN DEAL BOX

after William Tuffnell Le Queux

In that square, heavy box, of brown-stained deal, connected by its high-tension wires to three big industrial coils upon the table, was stored a force by which to bring Zeppelins to earth.

Zeppelins, floating high above, higher than aeroplanes! Zeppelins floating effortlessly through the night while aeroplane pilots keep to the ground unable to take off and land in darkness! Zeppelins floating too silently to be heard above the sound of the aeroplane's engines!

London, the greatest capital of civilized history, the hub of the whole world, seemed to lie at the mercy of the bespectacled night pirate who came and went as he pleased.

Those were no days for personal caution.

Claude and his chum, Teddy, both dressed in overalls and smoking gaspers, adjust a small vacuum tube within that mysterious looking wooden box, which is daily carried aloft in the fuselage of their aeroplane. They work in a shed populated by objects sure to puzzle the uninitiated: two lathes, a tangle of electric wires across the floor, great induction coils capable of fourteen-inch sparks, a small dynamo with petrol engine, and, upon the bench, strange-looking wireless condensers, radiometers, detectors.

As practical airmen, they have taken up the challenge of the Zeppelin seriously, devoting their meagre allowances toward combating the rapidly increasing peril of air attacks, and the result was the shed and the great mass of electrical apparatus it contained.

"Now let's put a test on it again—eh, Claude?" Teddy suggested. "Right ho!" acquiesced Claude.

RESTORATION

All I want is time to play,
to be with you always in sunlight-blanched dream,
in favourite coat and morning blanket memory,
on metal swings, the ones that looked like horses,
on the jungle gym fashioned as a fire truck—
these places are gone, but I see us revisit them,
outposts of unconquerable genius, of a world
where you live freely and to which I've been
repatriated by your grace.

Move on, if you will;
I'll steward the ill-assorted ark of stuffed beasts
and keep the plastic hoard. Once upon a time,
the things I loved as a child were boxed in a cellar,
underground as if already buried before me.
Then they were brought up for you,
and you delighted in them,
even the broken pieces.

THEY WILL KNOW US BY OUR HITS AND VIEWS

Beings of pure energy and purer math,
two-dimensional, flashes on screens,
they knew us by our hits and views,
thumbs-up icons clicked and ratings stars

scrolled across. Post nova, the earth
a cinder, but despite annihilation
of bodies and buildings, we'd left
artifacts for electromagnetic archaeology.

They recognized at once cartoons,
corporate logos, also clichés and puns,
loved dearly ciphers and indices. Only
photographs puzzled them. Snapshots

of flowers they perceived as obscure
hieroglyphs. So, too, prints of our naked
selves. What Rosetta Stone could they find
to unlock for them the word incarnate?

AM NOCTURNE

I foresee an extinction coming—indeed,
it has already come: the spectrum
once played upon with supple dials
is supplanted by channels fixed
and digital, like the shells of the atoms.

Multiply beyond all understanding
the quantity of these discreet compartments
for diversion and perhaps a system might result
with the charm of the maze—that trifle,
the fundamental despair of which is hid
by the apparent richness of its design.
But however splendid the tracery of its paths,
however pleasing the mental exercise derived
from its contemplation, one solution has been
established from the creation of this pretense.
The way is barred to chance, to creativity.
False starts and wrong turns amuse while working
the puzzle, comprise, in fact, its whole enjoyment
but possess no virtue, mere errors
adding nothing to the mock world. The maze
is singular, bereft of alternatives, of the true
pleasures of a world, and attempts with sham
complexity to please:
                              and such is the highest
rank to which the digital universe may aspire.
Too small, too straightforward, too knowable.
The mind surveys its contents in an instant,
foresees the limits of the available

enjoyment, as if gazing at a maze on which
the way is marked, all fun pre-empted.

                              I recall another world,
its compass more narrow, supposedly:
the AM radio band, scanned by the action
of fingers on the gently serrated edge
of a plastic disc protruding slightly
from the casing of a receiver or
on a fat knob erupting from a dashboard.

*

On the shelf nearest my pillow,
wedged between books, a radio:
its body white plastic, its mouth,
a black grill covering the speaker,
and its eye,
one elongated, rectangular pupil
beneath a lens tattooed with frequencies.

One ear protruded from the casing's left—
turn this disc and a fire red stripe
travelled smoothly across the AM band.

                          Baseball
and hockey broadcasts, first childhood favourites,
led me to others: radio plays
that came on after the game. Sometimes, startled
by hardwood creaking with the weather's changes,
I'd wake when sports and theatre were over,
and work the tuner, scanning silence and static
like an officer on a battleship

at signal post or sonar screen,
listening for code or submarine.

Now the band was like the night sky
beyond my native light pollution:
amid cardinal stars and planets,
distant, lesser points crowded,
their diamond edges dusked at times
by passing cirri.

To catch the team from across the lake
still at bat on the west coast—
its flagship station crackling
in one of the voids between the locals—
was to see Orion's sword hanging
from his brightly burning winter belt.

Back and forth I'd turn the dial—
my radio, a radio telescope—
aware that clear nights promised more:
high-pressure systems make floorboards sing,
and a richer nebula of frequencies be heard.

                    In the interstellar fuzz,
far off or less powerfully transmitted
signals would phase,
two or more alternating dominance,
even when I left the tuner at rest:
automatic collages of sound inviting intervention
by the artist-listener, a boy
leaning far out from the side of his bed,
sometimes dropping one arm to the floor for support
as he strained to reach the control.

*

How evacuated
that cosmos seemed years later as I punched
the scan button with my right index finger,
my left hand at ten o'clock on the wheel, one eye
on the deserted road, one on the liquid crystal
display that read out the coordinates, fixed and digital,
of a system in which all interstices had been annihilated.

A couple of passes were enough
to survey the possibilities
but I ran through them again and again, pausing
a shorter time on clear locks with each tour.
Long silences
as the receiver scrolled through ghost numbers
and short blurts
from destinations instantly recognized,
instantly rejected—I came at last
to associate the AM band with the sense of void.

I'd taken a job with the *Daily Northwestern*,
couriering artwork for tomorrow's campus news
from the union building to the printer downtown
at Fullerton and Ashland, forty-five minutes each way.
My motivations were simple: to drive a van;
to see the city by night.

Ashland was six lanes, all
empty, and black except for arrays of varied lights.
Traversing this space, deep and vacant, any encounter—
such as that of atoms to form all things
or of sound with an ear to make a song

or of some fragment of what has been uttered
with some other imagination to form a new
instance of speech—seemed impossible.

Except once:
heading downtown, I saw all southbound lanes
occupied by oncoming vehicles, the entire
breadth of that broad American avenue blocked,
three titanic street sweepers advancing
side by side as if one machine, relentless,
their pilots neither veering nor slowing
nor signalling to me what I should do.

At the last moment I had to turn
into the northbound traffic
and, while those lanes were clear,
behind me I heard a horn: a tail-finned
convertible with its top down despite the winter,
full up with revellers, who honked at me again
as their driver swung the space-age car hard
to port to get around—I hadn't checked
my blind spot.

                    After our brief convergence,
the only five satellites in the galaxy
dispersed: the convertible sped on, happy
to continue swerving, and disappeared;
the street sweepers continued their slow ascent
of the wrong side of Ashland
staying a long while in my rear-view mirror;
and I too continued, modestly over the limit,
straight down Chicago's coordinate plane
to twenty-four hundred north, sixteen hundred west.

*

AM 670 became my soundtrack, a joy
that maintained me during interstellar missions.
"The Music of Your Life" was the station's tag,
suggestive of catch-all playlists
and a patronizing, macabre conception
of audience: people whose lives are finished
and yet they linger, insomniac from maladies
of old age, shining electric blue
in the night-lights built into their clock radios' faces.
The tinny speakers on their bedside tables
are turned on low, but the announcer's voice resonates:
"You are listening to the music of your life."
And every time, I'd envision some figure,
angelic or demoniac, and in either case dressed
like a medical orderly, glimpsed darkly
as if in that dream-like state ascribed by some
to the early afterlife, and then consider
whether or not I could answer back:
"It is the music of my life."

                                    Perhaps my van
travelling faster than the speed of radio waves
had caught up to transmissions beamed into space
to introduce humanity to alien species
and I was arriving at strange planets
where the nostalgic was also the new — quaint
Einsteinian paradox. Or a Borgesian one:
the signals change as soon as I receive them;
whatever they were before, now they must be
interpreted in relation to all my life's music.

Insomniac listeners, fellow astronauts,
hurtling in starship beds,
sharing the space lanes, only ones to know
what I know at this moment,
in this vast void, no chance
for us to meet, except perhaps by strange
accident: what music do you seek?

Telstar,
our first artificial pulsar,
father to Earth's orbiting junk belt,
celebrated in an instrumental classic,
wishes to suggest its eponymous track—
"Telstar" by The Tornadoes.
Science fiction finds two expressions in music.
There is martial music, scored
for full orchestra in honour of glorious futures,
of the majesty
of scientists' genius and explorers' nerve.
And there is speculative music:
synthesized, electronic, made on principles,
an attempt to represent the otherness
of times to come with the means of today.
My theme song is perfect,
offers the satellite, a fanfare
but a fanfare for clavioline
and futuristic sound effects.

Another voice, darker—
the satellite's id—
counters that the true music of the space age
is a periodic bleep, the minimal melody
Telstar broadcast on its first flight.

We want no part of any of this, reply
my fellow travellers. We long for home,
and if our home is only this late night
then give us something to make us forget
that it is technology that bears us along,
technology that brings us music,
give us something sweet,
even if saccharine.

And I agreed with them, and wanted
their music, and kept it locked
on AM 670 whenever I made a run.

*

Each drive I listened for certain songs
and invariably I'd hear them, though shuffled
in different sets, at different times —
the station knew better than to disappoint.
There lingers in my ears
a "Trad" number, "Trad" here referring
to a British variation on old New Orleans jazz.
While played within the charm of that idiom,
this tune intended to evoke midnight
in Moscow by charting hints of klezmer
for banjo and for the interlocking horns —
trombone and trumpet but also clarinet.
Augmented seconds, leaps evocative
of gypsy steak and orthodoxy, feasts
scheduled by the Julian calendar,
and that touch of Transylvania that found
its way into the tango, all bopped
with Bourbon Street ebullience by an octet

of proper gents, who have arranged to step
up the counterpoint with each new chorus
in best Dixieland tradition.
Another song I waited on eulogized
the objects of backward-looking loves,
recalling in its lyric one particular
component of outmoded style: the round-
vowelled nonsense syllables
the backup singers used to fill out the sound—
sha-la-la and shing-a-ling-ling, the voice of a woman
herself dead from pop, proclaiming these figures
incantations capable of transporting
the listener to yesterday once more—
a sentiment worth logging for heavy rotation.
The third and final number in my short
hit parade was such a record as makes one think
that there are no distinctions between
art song, torch song, aria and ballad,
distinction perhaps in character but none
in the perfection each can attain,
a song a little dangerous while driving—
it threatens to occupy more of the mind
than the part left idle by navigation
of a straight and empty road. She sang from out
of the dashboard which through my hands
on the wheel had become a broadening
of my face, and the speakers extra mouths
through which I sang in this other, female voice,
backed up just to my taste by steel string
guitar, violin and harpsichord. How that song
seemed to come from within me!—even though
I imagined others lying awake
across Chicago thinking the same,

and others driving vans, desperate
for the next track, my song loved and cursed
for its maudlin dwelling in *temps perdu*,
in no way distinguished by either
its partisans or its detractors
from records in which I heard no redemption,
none of the orchestral restraint, none
of the lyrical surprise that has made
this particular oldie new for me
such a long, long time, past even
the vanishing of those hurts to which, I confess,
it once seemed to speak. The night was full
of fictions with whom I argued:
people who hear nothing,
who are content to possess
a familiar set of mediocre objects—
the death of pop,
the deathliness of their reactions to it.
But I was polarized, a pulsar
repelling masses of soupy material
while like-charged particles gravitated to me,
centre of a system where select reveries
of nostalgia and of love unrequited
helped form the exact figure of happiness,
a reconciliation of each person to the world.

*

                              I quit
after a run on which I discovered
AM 670 had changed format.
Advertisers perhaps saw potential
in one more talk station, expecting

late-night habitués dependent
on wakefulness and noise
to confirm their continued existence
would prefer incessant idle chat to music
that offered both the comfort and menace
of death's antechambers.

                        The digital tuner
became problematic again. How convenient
it had been to scan and fix with absolute
accuracy on 670. But in search of new
diversion, I rediscovered what a small fraction
of the multiples of ten between
530 and 1710 could lock,
and a manual search yielded little—
each lock was an outpost affording only
a narrow view of the airwaves.
Even when I did detect the trace
of some attractive signal,
I was prevented from knowing more
than its periphery.

                    One morning
I pulled the van into its place
in the concrete channel that sloped down
to the sunken loading dock. On AM 670,
a key figure in the greatest of political scandals
was hosting his new call-in show.
For a moment, he was an acid-tongued
commentator, savouring his own name's
notoriety as he repeated it to welcome
listeners back from every commercial break
and to greet each caller. His star burned out

with a turn of the key. I descended from
the high driver's seat, proceeded up the ramp
along one wall of the dock, deposited
the key in its secure return box, and
without having to re-enter the student union
for any old business, left my job
as a planet in a dying universe.

*

Years have passed, and tonight
as I wander through the dark rooms
of a new house, a radio is murmuring.
Earlier it bore you away to sleep,
and as I at last lie down
I begin to twirl the tuner—
there are still some such devices.
                                    Listen.
Stations are still transmitting:
not one old world has vanished, all persist.
Fleeing, perhaps, forever receding,
fading, even as we seek comfort in them—
part of what has been given us,
things we recognize and are bound to think of
as beautiful, even as we meet in them
our restlessness. We crave clarification:
a clear signal, but an elusive one,
a signal that would transcend or encompass
chaotic abundance. Or failing that
we wish for mastery:

prophecy of annihilation
that subordinates them to us,
establishes finally that they are for us,
and their transmissions will end when we will end.

DEATH DRIVE

Yes, I believe in the death drive,
in an instinct of destruction
directed against the external world.

We wish it would all stop
in five minutes, the entire fabric
of our moment, all the horror

and wonder of our materialism.
We don't fear the end, we fear
that we see no end: no shape

to our story, no renewal
for the earth, and so we wish
some cataclysm to overwhelm us.

Lynx and wolf and wild boar,
Eurasian brown bear, European bison,
Przewalski's horse and eagle owl

appear to thrive in the lush zone
of alienation around the ruined
Chernobyl power station,

and trees burst through rooftops
in ghost town Pripyat. But we
persist, able always to devise

repairs for the sarcophagus,
living just far enough away
in our new city, Slavutych, finding

biodiversity and birth rates
poor in the Red Forest despite
its Edenic aspect. What remains

uncertain is the state we seek:
though our elements have always,
existed, we haven't; irreducible,

we will never attain
the purity of inanimate things.
Yes, I believe in the death drive,

in the instinct to resolve
impasse and crisis by abandoning
ourselves to our own erasure.

But I don't buy it
as either sacrifice or nature.
This isn't a force equal and opposite

to other, creative urges, is not
part of some great balance;
this is our weakness and despair.

GARBAGE DAY

These are the days of our flesh: we cry often for things
which must, for now, be discarded. IBM 286, left curbside
in the rain, fat monitor on flat processor, head upon shoulders,
I shrouded you as best I could in a green-black bag,
but it wouldn't close over your components completely;
you wear a plastic poncho while dolefully awaiting
the trash pickup.
　　　　　　Remember 1991: precisely cut blocks
of Styrofoam secured the precious computer. Remember all
places the terminal's been set up, all fingers that have stroked
its keyboard and mouse, all faces the screen's reflected.
Let's agree to sympathize with each other's weaknesses: parting
with this obsolete device isn't straightforward. I confess,
not to abuses, not to negligence, but to memory of the delights
of this body, unblemished, corpse of one dead in youth,
kept well, but suddenly unable to boot—"recursive error"—
an ancient, and a lower class one at that, with a tiny defect
in the inner mysteries, not incurable, but uneconomical to fix.
Get a new one and scrap this shell, when the item's so plentiful.

If we were kings of this world, our armies would be fighting
to enslave experts and master wealth. But we are who we are,
on garbage day, fine observance for your passing on, IBM 286,
one of countless forms our dim godliness creates. I think of you
sadly, outside as afternoon darkens and dampens, object of a love
that must find fulfillment in another, endless and physical life.

SAXOPHONE

Facile to see the human form
extended in our instruments:
tennis rackets lengthen arms,
fork tines sharpen fingertips.
The saxophone is different:
arcing from mouth to abdomen
with pumping valves and ligaments
not appendage but exo-organ,
integral bodily system
performing its specific function
outside the confines of the skin,
as insects wear their skeletons.

IN PRAISE OF SHOGUN WARRIORS

Mecha is a genre of Japanese comics and cartoons that focuses on robots. *Gundam* (1979) broke Mecha into two sub-genres: the Super Robot genre, involving giant-sized robots, semi-mystical creations battling the villain's monster-minions; and the Real Robot genre, in which the robots are quasi-realistic weapons of war–armoured suits that are the future forms of tank and fighter planes. Shogun Warriors was the name of a line of toys and a comic book that brought the Super Robot genre to North America in the late seventies.

Mecha corruption
Mundane war on cosmic stage
Earth left far behind

Pathetic vision
Tomorrow's humanity
Walking fighter jets

Among the pilots
Prejudice, barracks' humour
Interplay of types

Old-fashioned GI nicknames
Genre anomie
They know "War is Hell"

I've no wish to see
Trench and tank drama transposed
To noiseless vacuums

Fantasy without
Fantasy, future
Without transfiguration

No more titans
The gritty played as the real
Moderns triumphant

Give us bright ancients
Skyline-scaled robots
Brave Raydeen, Mu's protector

Angular, alive,
Armour with jewel-toned sheen
Beetle-beautiful

Samurai armour
Pharoah sarcophagus head
Glorified body

Brave Raydeen, kouros, moai
In you our spirits
Find towering shape

Colossus, Titan
Your might may still be enjoyed
When Earth has been saved

All monsters redeemed
Paradise to live
Through you with you and in you

FUTURE-STATE TELEPHONY

Hearing isn't a sense separate from touch
but a subset defined by the invisibility of its works.
Players strum and strike and beat,
every noise shaped first by attack.
Later, phonographs, singing phrenologists,
must feel out the bumps of an album's groove
with their needle fingers.

Alarum from within a plastic form:
a device rings, and answering it,
I am caressed by a hand broadcast
into my living room, not a simulacrum
of a hand, nor any abstract hand
but a specific hand, that of my caller
at the other end of the apparatus,
her hand with me even while
it persists with her, its touch relayed
to me as bygone phones
once brought me the touch of her voice.

THE HEART'S HEALTH

The world blossoms from our eyes,
all except those plants that grow within
our beds of flesh: those blood roses
more anxious than all else: our hearts.

How to husband these pulsing flowers
that year-round form a red hot carpet
upon the earth, unseen except
by the special vision given our satellites?

Gardener's nemesis: species without rule,
one preferring sun, another shade;
delight also, that withered, dead leaves revive
unexpectedly, crimson and hale once more.

If you love one, end its anxieties,
even those that appear noble, occasions
for virtue: humour and courage are displays
of a heart's vitality, but not its health.

HOLY SATURDAY

The most worldly of days. By law,
the shops close reverently Good Friday and again
Easter Sunday, but it's not really a long weekend.
Saturday: business as usual, day of the dead god,
godless day with neither ritual nor scripture,
every other used to memorialize teaching and renewal
but this one, set apart for absence and waiting.

Numb shadows, the idle and inactive dead
in their lightless caves. All colours muted toward violet.
Darkness of an unilluminated room at night, blinds drawn,
no light source. Yet the eye sees: from somewhere,
through tortuous reflections, streetlight or starlight
activates the eye, and it sees, however dimly. Perhaps,
absolute darkness cannot exist except as an abstraction,
and the opened eye can never be without sight:
as in medieval science, vision projects from the eye.
In the caves of the waiting dead, the only music, only speech,
creakings, as of hardwood floors on nights of changing humidity,
and distant machine noises—refrigerators, furnaces,
suddenly audible when they shut down and fall silent.

Elsewhere, above ground: commerce, sport,
physical pleasure, not a thought for the dead or the supernatural.
The buds hold no promise of seasons: they burst,
the leaves spring forth, and there will be no new buds.
Come the winter, which must be the last one,
the leaves will go, the trees stand bare,
as the rotation of the earth and the circulation of our bodies run down,

and that's an end to it. Blank eyes,
struggling with the dimness of endless waiting,
just shy of absolute zero.

Our hope is absurd: to walk in a lane
where the gardeners keep at all times
a line of magnolias as they glory in each season.
In the first yard, one with small buds, fuzzy to the touch, joy of winter.
Next, one with full buds, some fractured by white and purple shoots.
Then one in full flower. And finally, one heartily leafed,
skirted at its base with fallen petals.
Absurd to hope for a day not only of rest but retreat.

SUMMER FADING AND THE FAIR

I'd like it to be forever the *fin de la saison*,
always an evening when surprisingly few people—
but still a good throng—have come out to the grounds.

It can never be what it was, which is all
I want it to be: to ride again the Alpine ride—
now utterly erased, its poles, its cable, its termini—
to see the lights I saw. To see the old stadium,
the tower that stood beyond its outfield, the *Haida*
in the harbour. I never crave any new diversions, want
what I had then. One improvement I might make:
to enjoy shooting water guns and whacking moles
for free and without any melancholy prizes—
let gaudy, oversized, stuffed things adorn
festive booths without encumbering the stroll
along the midway or haunting the backs of closets.

But these aren't my grounds:
will they be yours? Or is the fair lost?

We stop at a little circus, and my son's pulled up
on stage to play a tiger. The ringmaster
is suitably ancient to preside at such old-timey revels
and yet of such an age that when he was young
the great day of the circus had already died.

ON YOUR FIRST VISIT TO THE ZOO

We saw the aba aba,
electric fish, air breather,
in its customary tank
in an untrafficked corner
of the Africa pavilion,
grey body in grey water,
a few dark stones and leaves
for aquascape,
above the glass,
a vintage backlit sign,
glossy black background,
rainbow colours shining through
a cartoon schematic
of the creature's natural batteries.

We saw the aba aba,
electric fish, air breather,
the drama, the elegance,
of its single fin,
rippling along its back,
the whole length
of its Zeppelin form.

PARACHUTED CHERRY

In full bloom, embowering
your second-storey back window, as it had each spring,
the cherry's whited crown
that day was lifted by the storm's harrowing wind.
Uprooted, the tree ascended briefly before sprawling
across yard and fence. Admiral moths
on their migration swarmed its blossoms
while we awaited the disposal crew.
A giant of shade and beauty right up until it parachuted—
the technical term—it prefigures
its fellows along neighbourhood streets, fine to look at
but rotten inside; fluorescent orange dots
mark many soon to be chainsawed and chipped.
Mature and rich but quickly thinning,
our local canopy is a relic of an age
of attainment, an age that seems to end
in those stunted, nearly leafless locusts
propped up in holes in downtown concrete,
left to root in sun-starved sand beneath the sidewalk
amidst drain pipes and hydro lines.
But remember how the stripling oak
city workers planted in the bald
yard next to our old place made small gains each year—
before we left, it had risen above the light poles
to darken its lawn. Great trees still grow,
like the new "Indian Summer" crabapple
fruiting beneath your window tonight.

HILLSDALE

I didn't grow up in a splendid house
but it was a home of spaces I saw over and over,
spaces which remain and recur in my dreams.

Across town, in another house,
a man was wasting away, his wealth with him,
wealth that included the property we rented.

Now his dying body merges
with the place I thought of as my family's:
swollen like the bulges in the ceiling
where water that had leaked in through the roof
was trapped; skin peeling like the plaster that cracked,
exposing lathe; heartbeat irregular and muffled
like the drips caught in towels and pots on rainy days.

I've seen the house lately
with its new roof and windows, the junk tree gone
from where it had leaned against the facade,
a porch railing with no missing or broken slats,
the old garage out back razed and a pristine shed there:
the work of new money, which annihilated
the humble and dreaming spaces of my childhood
but also made of them
something that can live on in this world.

SONG: CITY, MIRROR, MOON

No use loitering
beneath the rented windows
we used to look out from:
you know we're not in there anymore.
No use hoping
to find our old haunts preserved
in the coffee-table book
Lost Landmarks of the City.
We've settled down,
we've chosen this town
but if we won't bury our hearts here,
then we're bound to disappear.
You're not some crumbling wall,
you are the genius of the place,
what the remnant takes with them
to found another capital.

No use covering
the mirrors of the medicine chest
or on the vanity
or above the mantelpiece.
No use ascribing
to the glasses a malevolence
that they do not possess:
it's just the light reflecting.
They used to ask,
who will you be,
now they say here's what you are,
here's all you'll ever see.
You're not some aging face;

you are a limitless world
that exists off to the side
even when no one's looking.

No use staring up
at the night sky or at a blank page
despairing that there's nothing new,
that all the heavens have been named.
No use compiling
all the images you have received
if they're only so much clutter,
just a weight you cannot bear.
We cast about
for words to fit our tune.
You fear you've been exhausted:
what's left to say about the moon?
You're not some poet's verse,
you are the satellite itself,
the source not the symbol,
what all seek to express,

a hope forever new,
the city, the mirror and the moon.

To sit again on a bench, one of a large edition
published by the city parks department,

in darkness rich with detail: small bulbs atop
regularly spaced poles along the lakeshore path,

the gloaming downtown some miles to your right—
which in that other home was south and now is west—

provide scant light, but light, once allowed in, gets
everywhere, spreading out, forever active, showing,

however dimly, tall grasses on this portion of the beach,
the horizon between black water and black sky.

To sit again on a bench with the wind made audible
by rising and falling white noise of waves coming in

and visible in the eruption and erosion of white peaks
in the water just before the shore. To know the tide

breaks also, the moon is new also, where you once sat.
To be calmed by the prospect, as befits great animals,

speechless, but with throat moist and tongue relaxed,
with thought freed from word or image, yet inclined

to create—a map of a borderless country that fades
with increasing distance from the lake—and to travel.

To sit again on a bench, to look southwest, vaguely
in the direction of another who looks northeast,

to look to another of your selves in the easy
familiarity of a bench in a night that finds voice—

your own, perhaps, in any case a voice within—
saying these lakes are one, these skylines one,

not that the world is one, but you've lived one life,
been one person, with a city by a lake for a homeland.

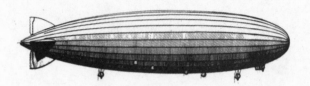

"An old photo of the Zeppelin that Goodyear flew out of Akron..." During the twenties and thirties, the Goodyear and Zeppelin companies were involved in a joint venture. Zeppelin personnel moved to Akron, Ohio, to help the Goodyear-Zeppelin Corporation build airships using Zeppelin Company patents, including the famous United States Navy airships, *Akron* and *Macon*.

"City Under an Epidemic": This poem began with a window display at the New Orleans Pharmacy Museum. The weather beacon described in the poem was inspired by the one atop the Canada Life Building on University Avenue in Toronto.

"Old Polonius": Some phrases at the beginning of the second stanza in this poem reference Henri Michaux's poem "Enigmas." "He had got into a hole and was waiting.... People threw stones at him, and he ate them" (as translated by Richard Ellmann).

"The Flamboyant Dictionary": This poem is rooted in Borges' "Dream-tigers": "I judged vast encyclopedias and books of natural history by the splendour of their tigers" (as translated by Mildred Boyer).

"During the Flood": "You shall take with you of every clean animal by sevens, a male and his female; and of the animals that are not clean two, a male and his female." Genesis 7:2. "...intricately woven in the depths of the earth..." Psalm 139:15 The phrase "living creatures" echoes passages in Ezekiel and Revelation.

"To Martial": The first-century Roman poet Martial was born in a colony in what is now Spain. *Liber Spectaculorum* is his first extant book of poems, published in AD 80 on the opening of the Colosseum. Although he went on to become famous as the master of the Latin epigram and as an observer of society in the early empire, little is known of his life during the fifteen years he spent in the capital before the appearance of *Liber Spectaculorum*.

"Makhmalbaf on the Iranian Cinema": Mohsen Makhmalbaf is a prominent Iranian filmmaker. Other Iranian directors are mentioned at the end of the poem. The notion of wanting to be played by someone good-looking is a reference to Makhmalbaf's film *A Moment of Innocence* (1995). The poem draws upon the entry for qasida in *The Princeton Encyclopedia of Poetry and Poetics* and also a newspaper article about contemporary Iranian cinema that is now lost to me but from which I took the quoted phrases "...virtue from necessity. Their style, artful and oblique, beloved of cineastes everywhere...unexpected byproduct of censorship." This poem was written for my friend Renato Umali's birthday in 2004.

"The Death of Robert Lowell": "the books are filled with the names of kings" is a line from Bertolt Brecht's "A Worker Reads History" (as translated by H.R. Hays). I first encountered it as an epigraph in Studs Terkel's *Working*.

"Ulysses": This poem references Tennyson's "Ulysses" but also a note in Christopher Ricks' edition of Tennyson: "[Hallam Lord Tennyson, Tennyson's son] comments: '....My father, like Eugammon, takes up the story of the further wanderings at the end of the Odyssey....The comrades he addresses are of the same heroic mould as his old comrades.' The last sentence is meant to meet the objection that Ulysses' companions were dead."

"The Port of London": Tilbury is the location of London's primary port. Tilbury docks were originally built in the late nineteenth century as an extension of the dock system that included the docks in London's East End. The port is the only part of the system that successfully adapted to changes in shipping, such as the use of containers. The upriver docks fell into disuse and have been the focal point of a number of high profile development and urban renewal projects, such as Canary Wharf.

"If the Child Could Be a Child Always": This poem owes much to the inspiration of Peter Handke's "Song of Childhood," best known as the opening narration in Wim Wenders' film *Wings of Desire* (1987).

"Movie Monster": The filmmaker imagined in the poem is a composite of director Ishiro Honda and special effects director Eiji Tsuburaya, who created *Godzilla* (1954). For the seminal Japanese monster film, Tsuburaya invented a new technique, sometimes referred to as suitmation, using an actor in a costume for giant monster sequences — as opposed to the use of models and stop-motion photography, as in *King Kong* (1933).

"The Saturday Penny": The title phrase comes from the Oxford English Dictionary's list of idiomatic phrases that include Saturday. "Saturday penny, a penny or small sum of money given to a child on Saturday as pocket money." This poem was first written as part of a sequence about the days of the week. Two other poems from this sequence appeared in my first book: "The Sunday Painter" and "I Consult Napoleon's Book of Fate." "Ben-Day dots" refers to a color printing process name after printer Benjamin Harry Day, Jr. It was commonly used in comic books during the 1950s and 1960s, and was famously appropriated as part of the pop-art style of painter Roy Lichtenstein.

"On Translating Spider-Man into Japanese": This poem refers to the debut episode of a Japanese live-action TV adventure series loosely based on the Marvel comic book character. The series aired in 1978 and 1979, but in recent years has been available as a cult curiosity on Marvel's website.

"Chapter III: The Brown Deal Box": William Tuffnell Le Queux (1864–1927) was a successful writer of mystery and espionage novels. An eccentric and a spirit of his age, Le Queux was also known as a journalist of gossip in the last days of Europe's pre-war aristocracy, an aviation buff and an early experimenter in radio. This piece references his book *The Zeppelin Destroyer* (1916), which I am also using as the basis of a novel.

"Song: City, Mirror, Moon": The second verse is influenced by Borges' poem "Mirrors" and the third verse by his poem "Moon," both of which appear in *Dreamtigers* (1960).

ACKNOWLEDGEMENTS

Thanks to Carleton Wilson for his friendship and collaboration, which have made this book a reality. Thanks to Roseanne Carrara, Albert Moritz, Theresa Moritz and Renato Umali for reading these poems in various forms over many years and for their invaluable contributions. Thanks to Pier Giorgio DiCicco, Richard Greene and Paul Vermeersch for reading the book prior to publication and for their support. Finally, thanks to Silas White and everyone at Nightwood Editions.

Thanks also to the editors of the following print and online journals in which some of the poems first appeared: *The Antigonish Review, Contemporary Verse 2, Descant, Encore Literary Magazine, Event, The Fiddlehead, Literary Review of Canada, PRISM, The Toronto Quarterly* and *Vallum.* "Movie Monster" will appear in *I Found It At the Movies,* edited by Ruth Roach Pierson (Guernica Editions, 2014).

Grateful acknowledgement is made to the Ontario Arts Council for a grant that supported the writing of this book.